No Need to Shout

a quick guide
to classroom discipline

John Robertson

Folens Publishers

Series Advisers

Gerald Haigh   Writer and Consultant in Education

Pauline Maskell   Secondary Head of Health Studies

John Sutton   General Secretary, Secondary Heads Association

Advisory Panel

Ruth Joyce   Adviser on Drugs and Health Education

Mike Kirby   Writer on Education

Terry Saunders   Secondary Head of Biology

Ann Morgan   Primary Deputy Headteacher

Elaine Wilson   Secondary Head of Science

ISBN: 1 85467 399 8

Folens Publishers
Albert House
Apex Business Centre
Boscombe Road
Dunstable LU5 4RL
Tel: 01582 472788   Fax: 01582 472575
Printed in Great Britain

Foreword

I like the idea of Quick Guides. Teachers need reliable
information and advice on a very wide range of
subjects related to their work and they need it to be
accessible and concise. This series attempts to meet
those needs by drawing on the knowledge of
experienced practitioners and presenting the essential
material in a format which facilitates rapid reference
and provides valuable action checklists.

I am sure that these guides will be useful to teachers, to
governors, to parents and indeed to all who are
concerned with the effective management of all
aspects of education.

John Sutton

General Secretary
Secondary Heads Association

John Robertson has been a teacher and an educational psychologist. He currently lectures on classroom management in teacher education programmes throughout the country.

Contents

Introduction

In contrast to what one might be led to believe from the publicity given to the most serious offences, such as violent and abusive behaviour, most pupils are very co-operative most of the time. However, teachers do have to deal with calling out, talking out-of-turn and disturbing other pupils on a daily basis, which can become very wearying. Pupils now appear more self assured and aware of their rights, expecting to have their say and be listened to: teachers therefore have the responsibility to ensure that the lively class does not degenerate into a disorderly mob dominated by a few irresponsible pupils.

The aims of this Quick Guide are to help teachers
- understand the nature of their relationships with pupils.
- reduce the opportunities and temptations for pupils to behave disruptively.
- deal effectively with low-level disruptions in non-confrontational ways and hence avoid provoking more serious challenges from pupils.

The text looks first at those factors which contribute to preventing disruption and then with ways in which teachers can respond to it more effectively.

Although the word 'student' is increasingly used in Secondary schools in preference to 'pupil' or 'child' which are more appropraite terms in Primary Schools, as this book is relevant for both Primary and Secondary school teachers, the latter terms have been retained.

Authority exists in a relationship and is an agreement between teachers and pupils.

Having authority is often confused with having power because both may be involved in managing pupils' behaviour. However, power is concerned with the ability to influence a person's behaviour by either rewarding or punishing their actions. With sufficient power we can make most people do what we wish, either because they fear what we will do to them if they don't comply, or because they want the rewards which we offer.

A moment's reflection will reveal that the use (or abuse) of power to make pupils comply has serious drawbacks:

- The legal powers available to teachers to reward or punish pupils' behaviour are very limited.
- All teachers have broadly the same powers but their authority with pupils varies considerably. Authority need not, and usually does not, result from simply having power.
- Pupils who are made to comply can develop hostile or resentful attitudes towards teachers.
- When the punishment can be avoided or the rewards are no longer available, the reason for complying has gone.

Authority is essentially an agreement between teachers and pupils about each having different rights in their relationship. As part of that agreement, pupils are expected to accept that teachers have limited legitimate powers to control outcomes for them.

Establishing one's authority
(continued)

In order for teaching and learning to take place, teachers have the right to expect that pupils will:

- Follow their work related instructions.
- Try to answer their work related questions.
- Give their attention as and when required.

Pupils should allow teachers to:

- Control the communication in the classroom.
- Control movement in the room.
- Decide on the appropriate content for the lesson.
- Organise the seating arrangements and grouping.

If pupils are expected to grant these rights, teachers have the responsibility to:

- Maintain a safe and orderly atmosphere.
- Treat pupils in a reasonable way.
- Plan their lessons.
- Try to present their lessons in an interesting and lively way.
- Present relevant work pitched at levels appropriate to the pupils' abilities and coherently explained.
- Mark pupils' work and give feedback on their progress.
- Have a good knowledge of the subject being taught.

In such ways teachers earn the authority they are claiming.

Teachers must create a context in which teaching and learning can take place.

To be regarded as a confident teacher one must act the part.

People act out their social positions relative to one another particularly when they meet on formal occasions. In their early meetings with classes teachers consolidate authority by acting in ways which express their senior position.

Teachers who are secure in their authority may:

- Remain relaxed, in posture, facial expression and tone of voice, particularly when challenged.
- Be able to sustain relaxed eye contact even when challenged.
- Move freely around the room and, when helping pupils, may rest on their tables and speak privately to them.
- Initiate contact with pupils and decide when the conversation has ended. Teachers can frequently be heard to say "Just a minute...I haven't finished yet".
- Choose to use pupils' first names or even more informal forms of address.
- Give instructions and ask questions.
- Ask pupils to come to them in order to speak to them.

Pupils are not likely to act in such ways towards teachers in the initial relationships but if they do they are claiming to be on a more equal footing and teachers must decide whether or not to bring this into question.

 No Need to Shout: a quick guide to classroom discipline

Very young children may sometimes treat teachers as they do their parents, seeking a cuddle or expecting to get their attention on demand, but by the age of seven most have learned that their relationships with teachers are less personal. However, teachers may still express warm, caring attitudes towards them, for example by holding them by the hand or by placing a hand on the back of a child's head when congratulating or comforting him or her. Such parental gestures decrease as children get older and by the Secondary stage pupils are usually only touched by teachers on the upper arm or back and male teachers avoid touching female pupils altogether.

Education is not something teachers do to pupils, it is something they share with them.

Pupils are more likely to co-operate with teachers who are genuinely concerned about their educational welfare and are interested in them as people. If they dislike teachers they will resist following instructions and take every opportunity to annoy them, whereas a disapproving glance from a teacher one likes will usually be heeded.

Though it is a mistake to solicit friendship, experienced teachers allow more informal, friendly relationships to develop naturally and always try to work with their pupils rather than against them, particularly when trying to deal with inappropriate behaviour.

Teachers who get on well with pupils:

- Take an interest in their lives outside school.
- Greet them by name and smile in a friendly manner.
- Share humour with them when appropriate.
- Acknowledge their special occasions such as birthdays, and encourage the group to share in each individual's successes and disappointments.
- Use language which identifies them with rather than segregates them from pupils (we, our, us).
- Support sporting, social and extra curricular activities which allow more informal equal relationships with pupils.
- Listen to and consult with them at appropriate times about their work and behaviour.
- Take disciplinary action in a fair and professional way when necessary.

Developing good relationships
(continued)

Primary school children often seek friendly relationships with teachers and the daily contact helps in this process, but adolescents primarily want acceptance from their peers, and this, together with less frequent and prolonged contact with a particular teacher, tends to limit the development of close relationships.

An essential expression of a caring relationship from all teachers is to try to ensure that pupils progress in their learning.

Choosing the right methods

Teaching has come a long way since the days of endless 'chalk and talk' and now a variety of methods are used to help pupils learn. We can categorise these methods in various ways, for example by considering the *type of activity* being carried out, e.g.

PRESENTATION – where the teacher transmits information, ideas or skills by 'telling and showing'. (lecture and demonstration)

INTERACTION – where knowledge and experience are shared between the teacher and pupils, using questioning, discussion and structured activities.

SEARCH – where pupils explore and discover for themselves by problem solving, investigations, experiment and research.

Whereas 'Presentation' is centred on the teacher, 'Search' emphasises the pupils' active role, which is another approach to categorising teaching methods.

The key question however is *which methods are most appropriate to the learning outcomes the teacher is trying to facilitate?* As a general guide, the learning outcomes can be matched to the type of activity in the following ways.

- KNOWING THINGS (terms, facts, sequences), promoted by *repetition, mnemonics,* and *jingles* to enhance **rote memory.**

- UNDERSTANDING THINGS (meanings, principles, processes), promoted by *explanation, questioning, problem solving* and *discovering* to produce **meaningful learning.**

- BEING ABLE TO DO THINGS (methods, skills, procedures), promoted by *examples, demonstrations,* and *supervised practice* to improve **competence** and **performance**.

- DEVELOPING ATTITUDES AND FEELINGS ABOUT THINGS (interests, choices, judgements), by giving and reflecting on *personal experiences, discussions, videos, visits* and *role play* to influence **motivation** and **actions.**

Decide on the learning outcomes one is trying to promote and choose effective ways of achieving them.

Choose methods which pupils are most likely to co-operate with, be motivated by and learn best from.

In addition to the type of learning outcomes we hope to achieve, other factors will affect our choice of methods.

☐ TIME AVAILABLE. 'Telling' takes far less time than letting students discover for themselves.

☐ NEED TO MAINTAIN PUPILS' ATTENTION. Being actively engaged in a variety of ways can help sustain one's interest. One method used for too long can become boring.

☐ NATURE OF THE SUBJECT. What is the balance of facts, concepts and skills? (Compare Mathematics, Modern Languages and Information Technology)

☐ RESOURCES AVAILABLE. 'Search' or pupil centred activities usually require greater resources.

☐ GROUP'S CHARACTERISTICS, i.e. age, abilities, motivation, experience. For example, learning by listening is easier for motivated and intellectually able pupils; interactive and search methods can be more easily disrupted if pupils are so inclined; pupils may need time to adjust to, and make the most of different ways of working.

☐ TEACHER'S RELATIVE STRENGTHS, i.e. lecture, explanation, group work, demonstration. If your methods are working, be careful as you try to improve them.

If we can choose the right methods to interest pupils and enhance their learning, they in turn will develop positive attitudes towards the subjects and behave co-operatively.

Learning is an active process. However we cannot see whether pupils are mentally engaging in the process simply by observing what they are doing. Those apparently listening to a teacher's explanation or reading books may be daydreaming, and even if they are carrying out a practical task they may be attending to very superficial features of the process.

The major task for teachers is therefore to capture pupils' attention which will not only maximise the possibility of their learning but will also reduce the likelihood of disruption. People watching favourite television programmes are reluctant to be drawn away even when visitors call and would certainly not choose to switch off without very good reason. In a similar way, pupils who are interested in their work are less likely to initiate or be drawn into any disruptive behaviour.

THE SPANISH INQUISITION

A teacher's enthusiasm and energy are contagious and likely to be caught by the pupils.

Pupils are more likely to become involved in their work when:

- ☐ Teachers present their subjects in an involved, enthusiastic manner and avoid ponderous and rambling explanations.
- ☐ Links are made to their personal experiences or interests.
- ☐ The activities and teaching methods are varied.
- ☐ They have the opportunity to participate in activities and contribute to discussions.
- ☐ The work presented arouses their curiosity or challenges their views.
- ☐ They understand the purpose of the work they are asked to do.
- ☐ The work targets set are challenging but achievable.
- ☐ They are seated in ways which are appropriate to the type of communication necessary for the activity. Table arrangements encourage pupil interaction; rows reduce it.
- ☐ Teachers show genuine interest in their contributions and value the products of their efforts.

Enthusiastic and committed teachers can be inspirational to their pupils.

Minimising 'dead-time'

Disruption does not occur randomly throughout the lesson: pupils are more likely to lose attention, chatter or fool around when they are waiting for the next thing to do or for the next idea to be presented.

Opportunities for disruption mainly occur when

- the teacher arrives late or does not start the lesson promptly. One should establish routines for such occasions but try not to leave the class unsupervised. Lessons should begin on time, with a sense of urgency.
- some pupils do not have the required books or equipment. Keep spares, materials and resources if possible and establish fair consequences for regular negligence by pupils.
- pupils are unsure of what they should be doing or how it should be done. Explanations and instructions should be as clear and concise as possible, and written on the board for their reference.
- the focus of the lesson is interrupted. Try to minimise any source of distraction or delay such as lengthy public reprimands when correcting behaviour or inefficient management of the transitions from one activity to another (e.g. from listening to an introduction to beginning group work).
- there is excessive or unnecessary movement in the room. Establish clear rules and procedures to keep essential movement orderly.

The devil finds work for idle hands (and minds).

- some pupils have finished the set work and have nothing to do. Have challenging follow-up activities prepared for those who have satisfactorily completed their work.
- insufficient time has been allowed to end the lesson in an orderly way. When the pupils are ready to leave, use any spare time to recapitulate the main points of the lesson and check if these have been understood.

When pupils are working in groups, a method most frequently used in Primary schools, it is important to discourage those who would let others do all the work by setting them specific targets and frequently checking their efforts. If pupils are engaged in their work they are less likely to try to distract others and are themselves less easily distracted.

Praise to prize: which system?

It is widely acknowledged that praise is not only more likely to create better relationships than correction but is also more effective in reducing disruption. The principle of *catching them being good* instead of just watching out for misbehaviour seems straightforward, but the manner in which praise is given is critical, particularly with older pupils.

'Praise' may cause embarrassment or be perceived by pupils as insincere or patronising if

- *it is given publicly to set an example to other pupils* and hence imply their inadequacies. The pupil is thus singled out from the peer group who may then resent the 'teacher's pet', the 'swot' or the 'toad'. Young children are less prone to this reaction as most still want to please the teacher, but as they grow older, acceptance by their peers becomes paramount. Giving praise **privately** acknowledges this fact.

We must take care not to appear patronising when we praise pupils' efforts.

Praise should show pupils that their efforts are valuable and appreciated and give them a greater sense of self-esteem.

- *the teacher evaluates performance and sets standards.* Evaluating pupils' efforts and showing ways in which they can improve are essential aspects of a teacher's role. However, if one does this in a patronising 'Good boy, I'm very pleased with you' manner, it may not express genuine appreciation of their work (though younger pupils may not realise this, being keen to please the teacher). When we judge other people's efforts, 'That's a great improvement on the work you did yesterday', and set standards, 'Make sure you keep it up', we are also expressing our own superiority in relation to the pupil. A teacher would be unlikely to say to the Headteacher, 'That was a much better assembly you gave this morning. Well done, keep it up'.

- *it is focused in general terms on the pupil* rather than specifically on what he or she has done, e.g. 'That's a lovely story. You are a clever girl', instead of 'What a beautiful description. You must have been thinking of somewhere you love to visit.'

Praise should express the teacher's positive **reaction** to what pupils have done and not be a response calculated to manipulate them in some way. Pupils' self-esteem is enhanced when teachers show their *appreciation, thanks, admiration* or *pleasure*. It should be given for genuine effort or achievement because rather than just feeling pleased, they should have something to feel pleased about.

Giving rewards or prizes is more controversial, particularly for improvements in behaviour or attendance, but most pupils can be motivated by offering an appropriate incentive.

A reward system usually involves the distribution of house points or stickers for work or good behaviour, which are accumulated either for school competitions on an individual, form or house basis, or which eventually can be exchanged for more tangible rewards.

Critics of such approaches warn that we may be teaching pupils that acceptable behaviour and intellectual effort are only a means to a materialistic end rather than being valuable for their own sake, i.e. token rewards lead to token learning.

If a reward system is used, the following features are important:

- It should be given a '*high profile*' within the school.
- The 'currency' (house points, stickers, badges, merits, certificates) should be *attractive*.
- The rewards should be *accessible to all pupils*, not just the high achievers.
- The distribution of the tokens should be *fair*, with all staff giving similar amounts for behaviour, effort and achievement.
- Staff should award the tokens in the form of a *gift* rather than as a payment, to avoid the development of 'pay bargaining', with pupils making their behaviour conditional on receiving satisfactory rewards.

Rewards should be visible, tangible, attractive and accessible.

A wide range of prestigious, social and personal incentives may be used separately or together to back-up a token reward system.

Status enhancing or prestigious incentives include

- congratulations from the Headteacher
- asking parents to telephone the teacher, who then describes the pupil's success
- letters of commendation to parents
- displays of work and achievements in 'public' areas of the school.

The intention is to *celebrate the pupil's success.*

Social incentives involve contributing the individual 'earnings' towards a group effort.

- The teacher agrees to give a class privilege (e.g. visit, free choice sessions, no uniform day, party) when the form reaches a particular target total. In Primary classes the target can be to fill a jar with marbles or dried peas, which the teacher gives in addition to, or instead of, a personal merit. The pupils thereby donate the fruits of their efforts to the whole class.
- The school sponsors forms or houses by agreeing to match their totals with donations to nominated charities.

Individual incentives take the form of exchanging tokens for

- entertainment, 'fast food' or concert vouchers for either pupils or parents
- money
- tickets for a monthly or termly lottery offering major prizes. Some Secondary schools allocate a considerable sum of money annually to provide attractive and valuable prizes which pupils can win for themselves or their parents in this way, and claim this produces radical improvements in standards of work and behaviour.

Younger children respond well to tokens of appreciation such as stickers, stars and smiley faces, but older pupils regard them as childish without the back-up of more tangible rewards.

Remaining vigilant

A quality that successful teachers show is what one American researcher described as 'withitness' – seeming to have eyes at the back of their heads – so that they are aware of the first signs of disruption almost before it occurs. It can then be nipped in the bud with a warning or low key intervention far more easily than when the disruption has taken place and begun to spread. Teachers who fail to take early action when it is called for give the impression of either incompetence, in not realising the need for action, or lack of confidence in their ability to deal effectively with it.

A stich in time...

What successful teachers have is probably not a 'sixth sense' but the experience to spot the early warning signs of pupils going off-task. They distinguish those incidents which could lead to serious disruption and call for direct action, such as a disciplinary intervention or changing the activity, from those which are likely to be short-lived and can be tactically ignored. Typical early warning signs are:

- Increase in the volume and particularly the pitch of the noise in an area of the room when pupils are working.
- Increase in movement. If this is widespread it can indicate that the students are losing concentration on the teacher's delivery, or have completed work which has been set. It can also be seen when pupils anticipate the end of a lesson.

Showing an awareness and quiet disapproval of what is happening, or about to happen, may be sufficient to stop it.

In deciding whether or not to intervene, experienced teachers consider:

- ☐ Are the pupils attempting to conceal their actions?
- ☐ Do they seem to be carefully checking on the teacher's position in the room?
- ☐ Do they adopt 'frozen' postures or other attempts at innocence when the teacher unexpectedly looks their way?

Such incidents, if not dealt with, are likely to spread and develop into a serious threat to the teacher's authority, so one should bear in mind:

- ☐ Is the incident a private, good natured event?
- ☐ Is it clearly not intended to involve pupils other than those directly concerned nor to test the disciplinary skills of the teacher?

Private chatting or occasional 'mucking about' are normal and not intended to present a serious threat to the teacher's authority and a disapproving look is usually sufficient to restore order.

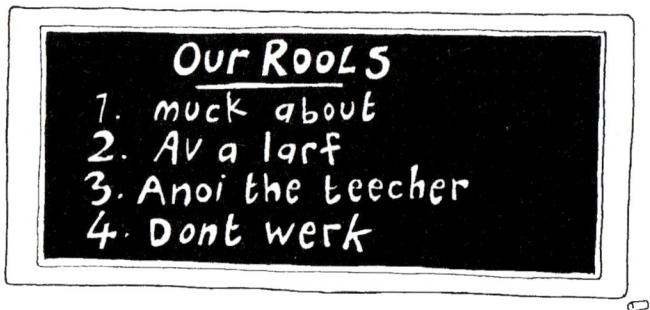

OUR ROOLS
1. muck about
2. Av a larf
3. Anoi the teecher
4. Dont werk

Personal responsibility

We can emphasise the responsibility that pupils have for their own actions by:

☐ Negotiating 'our' classroom rules to give the class a sense of ownership and control of their own conduct.

☐ Presenting choices to pupils rather than issuing intimidating threats. Rather than threaten 'If I see you talking again, I'm going to move you!', we can emphasise personal responsibility by saying 'It's up to you: you can either choose to work quietly here or I shall have to move you.'

☐ Giving pupils time and space to follow our instructions rather than standing over them until they have 'obeyed'. However *always follow-up* if they do not comply in a reasonable time.

☐ Avoiding giving instructions in imperative forms, as orders, unless requests and hints have been ignored. Even then, one should remain calm and professional in manner, implying 'You know you should do this', rather than 'You had better do this or else'.

If we try to force pupils to comply, we take over responsibility for their actions, a step which should only be taken in extreme circumstances such as when their behaviour threatens their own or others' safety. Young children should learn to *co-operate* with teachers, rather than to *obey* them.

We should always emphasise to pupils that they are responsible for their own behaviour and the consequences that result from it.

Everyday minor offences should be handled in unobtrusive, non-confrontational ways.

Most pupils behave appropriately most of the time, and minor 'offences' such as talking out-of-turn, calling out and disturbing others, though extremely common, are seldom carried out with any disruptive or malicious intent. Teachers may sometimes let such incidents pass, choosing to attend to those who are behaving appropriately in the hope that the offenders take the point, or will intervene in a low-key private manner to remind them to check their behaviour.

The features of such interventions are:

- They are private in nature. The teacher first gets the pupil's attention, calling him or her by name if necessary, then may give a *non-verbal reminder*, such as raising one's eyebrows in a questioning manner, or shaking one's head to indicate 'No'.
- They imply that pupils really know what they should be doing, sometimes being carried out *incidentally*, while the teacher apparently attends to another matter. For example, while speaking to the class the teacher might remove a pen from a pupil who is writing.
- They give the impression that the teacher *expects the pupil to co-operate*. Instructions may be phrased as questions, 'Can you take your seat please Adrian', or as hints, 'I think some people could be making more effort.'

By giving corrections in such ways, the teacher emphasises the co-operative nature of the relationship.

Intervening professionally

When gentle reminders are not heeded or the offence is more serious, we need to intervene directly with the pupil. The outcome of this intervention is more likely to be affected by *how* we behave and speak than *what* we say or do.

In contrast to giving praise, correcting pupils' behaviour should be carried out in a professional, detached manner rather than in a personal, involved way. If one either behaves aggressively or appears unsettled, the episode is likely to develop into a personal battle, particularly when carried on publicly in front of other pupils.

A professional manner is expressed by:

- Remaining calm and sustaining relaxed eye-contact with the pupil.
- Avoiding frowning, glaring or any other threatening expressions.
- Using open-handed palm-down gestures and not pointing or 'stabbing' at the pupil.
- Giving clear instructions in a relaxed assertive tone without raising one's voice.
- Being close enough to speak privately if possible but without invading the pupil's personal space.
- Avoiding threatening body postures such as hands on hips or thrusting one's chin forward.
- Treating the pupil with respect. Deal with the behaviour and not the pupil and avoid personal remarks or dismissive attitudes (e.g. 'You can't keep your mouth shut for a minute, can you?' or 'I don't care whether you're tired....').

Teachers' manner and language should clearly express confidence in their professional responsibility to deal with pupils' behaviour.

Pupils' behaviour must conform to a few basic rules or codes of conduct concerning orderly communication and movement, fair and considerate treatment of other pupils and their property, and following instructions from teachers. In addition there may be school rules relating to issues such as eating and dress.

Teachers may choose whether or not to make classroom rules explicit but, stated or unstated, *it is essential that they ensure that pupils behave in accordance with them.* For example, a teacher who resists interruption from those who call out but gives way to those who indicate they wish to speak is implicitly teaching a rule about communication, whereas one who states such a rule (e.g. 'Raise your hand if you wish to speak') but does not act to enforce it, teaches pupils to ignore it.

In deciding whether or not to state rules explicitly one should bear in mind that the more they are proclaimed and stressed, the greater is the implication that they will be needed: the less they are publicised, the more one implies that pupils already know how to behave and can be trusted so to do.

Establishing classroom rules
(continued)

In most schools a clear statement of rules is usually felt to be necessary and the following general principles can be helpful.

- Rules should have an underlying **rationale.** Those which do not are difficult to justify when challenged, e.g. regarding details of dress or personal appearance. Most rules are made to protect pupils' rights, e.g. to learn and to be safe.

- When possible they should be **negotiated** with the pupils as they will then be more likely to keep 'our' rules. Some rules may not be negotiable but pupils will usually draw up very similar rules to those which teachers require.

- They should be **brief, few in number** and **clear** so that they can easily be learned.

- When possible, rules and instructions should be phrased in **positive** and **user friendly** forms
  e.g. 'Follow the teacher's instructions without argument'
  'Take your turn when you wish to speak without interrupting others'
  'Treat others with consideration and courtesy'
  'This classroom is an eating, drinking and chewing-free zone'

Pupils can illustrate the class rules they have helped to make and these can be displayed in preference to dull, written lists. This is particularly important for most Primary school children, who take more notice of pictures than just words.

School rules should usually be *enforced by all teachers*. If some turn a blind eye when rules are broken it becomes harder for others to enforce them.

We should be prepared to justify our rules to pupils at an appropriate time but not necessarily on every occasion that pupils choose to challenge them.

Many educators recommend we follow the 'law of least intervention' by beginning with the least intrusive measure sufficient to deal with the pupil's offence and, if the behaviour in question continues, progressing in a series of planned steps before giving a related consequence For example,

1. Give low-key reminder.
2. Clearly tell the pupil what you want them to do.
3. Present the pupil with a choice either to follow your instruction or to incur the related consequences.
4. Give the related consequences.
5. Resume normal relationship with the pupil.

Examples of related consequences would be:

- Clearing up or tidying classroom for dropping litter or misuse of resources.
- Completing work during the lunch-hour for wasting time during the lesson.
- Moving seat for talking with neighbour.
- Removal from the room for persistent disruptive behaviour sufficient to impede teaching and learning (to be used only as a last resort and preferably carried out by another teacher).

An alternative approach involves progressively increasing one consequence, usually a detention, in no more than five stages, e.g.

First offence	verbal reminder
Second offence	pupil's name noted, 5 minutes detention
Third offence	10 minutes detention
Fourth offence	20 minutes detention
Fifth offence	20 minutes detention interview with senior teacher or removal from class

Adopting a planned approach enables teachers to remain calm and professional when addressing pupils' behaviour as they should always know what to do next and therefore should feel less threatened.

Where the general standards of conduct in a school are felt to be unsatisfactory and the everyday low-key reminders and unsystematic corrections and consequences are not effective, many schools turn to official school behaviour policies.

If we think of pupils in schools playing 'The Learning Game', as with any game or sport, they not only need to know the rules but also the consequences that follow when rules are broken. Rules and consequences need to acquire an 'official' status whereby teachers, like referees, are seen as having to enforce them *as a professional duty*, so that pupils are clear about the predictable risks they run.

We can impart an official status to rules and consequences by:

- ☐ Displaying them clearly in classrooms and around the school.

- ☐ Publicising them in booklets to parents and governors.

- ☐ Explicitly teaching them to pupils and periodically checking to see that they have been learned and remembered.

- ☐ Ensuring that all staff enforce them fairly and consistently.

- ☐ Enforcing them in a professional, not personal manner.

Such systems allow pupils to avoid predictable consequences by following teachers' instructions. An unexpected consequence, particularly if perceived as relatively severe, is likely to be regarded as personal and unfair and can worsen relationships with the pupil making further problems more likely.

Ensure that consequences are inevitable rather than severe.

Some schools use terms and symbols borrowed from sports, such as the yellow and red card system in association football, which emphasises their official status. Pupils see famous sports stars obeying such symbols and are therefore likely to follow suit. Unlike referees, however, teachers should always have the discretion not to enforce consequences if they feel there are extenuating circumstances, but doing this frequently will weaken the 'official' nature of one's actions.

The 'game' analogy can be extended with younger children to encourage them to

- turn up to the game on time.

- come with the right kit, ready to play.

- not be beaten by their opponents, e.g. Day Dreamer, Larry Lazy, Charlie Chatterbox, Gary Give-up. (Avoid first names of children in the class.)

- avoid fouling (breaking rules).

- score their own personal learning goals and help the rest of the team score theirs.

And remember, *the referee's decision is final*!

Such 'official' systems are always used in conjunction with the systematic application of praise and rewards.

When pupils really enjoy the Learning Game, the referee is seldom needed. The teacher can concentrate on being the coach and trainer.

Fix the problem, not the blame.

Rather than simply using punishment in the hope of deterring future misbehaviour, teachers frequently discuss the problem with pupils to help them change their attitudes and behaviour.

In one's meeting with the pupil to discuss the problem (eg, during a 'detention'):

Share responsibility

- Keep the meeting informal to allow a relaxed and frank discussion.
- Reach a clear understanding about what the problem is.
- Focus on 'our' problem rather than 'your' problem or worse still, imply the pupil is the problem.

Confront the problem

- Use discussion, reasoning, role play or simulation to let the pupil have some experience of the way their behaviour affects you and other pupils.
- Take the pupil's view of the matter seriously, and try to accommodate any reasonable wishes or requests.

Helping persistent offenders
(continued)

Decide on a plan of action

- Reach agreement on an achievable target in a given period of time.
- Show your willingness to help the pupil achieve the target, e.g. offer incentives for success; agree on private reminders rather than public reprimands; offer the assistance of another pupil to help them keep to their plan of action.

Be clear about further consequences

- Make sure the pupil knows exactly what will follow in the next stage of the process should the offences continue.
- The subsequent stages in the process should become more formal, involving parents and senior teachers, reflecting the increasing seriousness of the matter.

The aim of such discussions is to continue to *work with, rather than against the pupil* to overcome the problem. 'Disciplinary' interviews frequently only consolidate hostile attitudes.

What happens?

Why is it a problem?

What are we going to do about it?

What will happen next if it continues?

A sense of solidarity and common purpose in the school community begins with the staff.

Teachers need to present a unified front not in opposition to pupils but in fulfilling the roles expected of them in the school community.

A sense of common membership is felt in those schools where the staff

- socialise during breaks and lunch hours in the staffroom rather than remain isolated or confined to a small faculty group.
- support and contribute to assemblies, sports and social events for pupils and staff.
- contribute to extra-curricular clubs and activities.
- celebrate one anothers' special occasions.
- avoid critical gossip with pupils and teachers about their colleagues.

One should follow recognised professional procedures in reporting matters relating to unprofessional conduct or other unacceptable behaviour. When in doubt, consult a senior colleague.

There are many occasions when teachers need to be able to rely on their colleagues' support in dealing with difficult problems.

Teachers can help one another by:

- Jointly teaching with a vulnerable colleague to strengthen their authority.
- Taking a colleague's class to allow them some time to work with difficult individuals or groups to overcome problems.
- Mediating in disputes between colleagues and pupils to help them resolve their problems.
- Contributing to school behaviour policies such as the planned removal and supervision of disruptive pupils from colleagues' classrooms.
- Enforcing the school rules anywhere on the premises, not 'turning a blind eye'.

Recommended reading

Mick McManus, *Troublesome Behaviour in the Classroom*, Routledge, 1989.

Sean Neil and Chris Caswell, *Body Language for Competent Teachers*, Routledge, 1993.

John Robertson, *Effective Classroom Control* (3rd Edition), Hodder & Stoughton, 1996.

Bill Rogers, *You Know the Fair Rule*, Pitman, 1990.

Bill Rogers, *Behaviour Recovery*, Pitman, 1994.

Folens resource packs:

Anti-Bullying: A Drama Resource Pack
Penny Casdagli
ISBN 1 85467 266 5

Anti-Bullying: A Whole School Approach
Maggie Stockton
ISBN 1 85467 278 9

Drama and Personal and Social Education
Ruth Hilton and Claire Hill
ISBN 1 85467 227 4

Raising Self-Esteem: 50 Activities
Murray White
ISBN 1 85467 231 2

Rights and Responsibilities
Michael Kirby
ISBN 1 85467 187 1

Self-Esteem: Its Meaning and Value in Schools, Set A
Murray White
ISBN 1 85467 253 3

Self-Esteem, Its Meaning and Value in Schools, Set B
Murray White
ISBN 1 85467 263 0

Self-Esteem Solutions
Edited by Murray White
ISBN 1 85467 271 1

Study and Learning Skills
Butcher, Cox, Cutter, Lister, Moor, O'Keefe and Renfrew
ISBN 1 85467 261 4

Folens resource packs are:

✓ **Fully photocopiable**

✓ **Ready for use**

✓ **Flexible**

✓ **Clearly designed**

✓ **Tried and tested**

✓ **Cost-effective**

The Quick Guide series from Folens

Quick Guides are up to date, stimulating and readable A5 booklets, packed with essential information and key facts on important issues in education

Health education

Drugs Education for children aged 4–11: A Quick Guide
Janice Slough
ISBN 1 85467 326 2

Drugs Education for children aged 11–18: A Quick Guide
Janice Slough
ISBN 1 85467 324 6

Alcohol: A Quick Guide
Dr Gerald Beales
ISBN 1 85467 300 9

Smoking Issues: A Quick Guide
Paul Hooper
ISBN 1 85467 309 2

Sex Education: A Quick Guide for Teachers
Dr Michael Kirby
ISBN 1 85467 228 2

Sex Education for children aged 4–11: A Quick Guide for parents and carers
Janice Slough
ISBN 1 85467 312 2

Sex Education for children aged 11–18: A Quick Guide for parents and carers
Janice Slough
ISBN 1 85467 313 0

Eating Disorders: A Quick Guide
Dee Dawson
ISBN 1 85467 321 1

Stress Management: A Quick Guide
Stephen Palmer & Lynda Strickland
ISBN 1 85467 316 5

Career enhancement

Assertiveness: A Quick Guide
Chrissie Hawkes-Whitehead
ISBN 1 85467 305 X

Counselling: A Quick Guide
Chrissie Hawkes-Whitehead
and Cherry Eales
ISBN 1 85467 302 5

Problem People and How to Handle Them: A Quick Guide
Ursula Markham
ISBN 1 85467 317 3

Class and school management

Bullying: A Quick Guide
Dr Carrie Herbert
ISBN 1 85467 323 8

Primary School Inspections: A Quick Guide
Malcolm Massey & David Lee
ISBN 1 85467 308 4

Grief, Loss and Bereavement: A Quick Guide
Penny Casdagli & Francis Gobey
ISBN 1 85467 307 6

Safety on Educational Visits: A Quick Guide
Michael Evans
ISBN 1 85467 306 8

Equal Opportunities: A Quick Guide
Gwyneth Hughes & Wendy Smith
ISBN 1 85467 303 3

Working in Groups: A Quick Guide
Pauline Maskell
ISBN 1 85467 304 1

Organising Conferences and Events: A Quick Guide
David Napier
ISBN 1 85467 314 9

Working with Parents: A Quick Guide
Dr Michael Kirby
ISBN 1 85467 315 7

Truancy: A Quick Guide
John Jones
ISBN 1 85467 319 X

Governor Training: A Quick Guide
Michael Booker
ISBN 1 85467 320 3

© Folens **No Need to Shout: a quick guide to classroom discipline**

For further information

For further details of any of our publications mentioned in this Quick Guide, please fill in and post this form (or a photocopy) to:

Folens Publishers
Albert House
Apex Business Centre
Boscombe Road
Dunstable LU5 4RL

Tel: 01582 472788
Fax: 01582 472575

Name ....

Job Title ....

Organisation ....

Address ....

....

Postcode ....

Tel No. ....

Fax No. ....

Please send me details of the following publications:

Notes

© Folens **No Need to Shout: a quick guide to classroom discipline**

Notes

Notes

© Folens **No Need to Shout: a quick guide to classroom discipline**